This book belongs

to ___________________________

Dinosaur Publications

Blood and Thunder

Investigator's Notebook

by Josie Karavasil
illustrated by Hilary Evans

Published by Dinosaur Publications Ltd, Over, Cambridge, Great Britain.

ISBN 0 85122 409 1 (paperback)
ISBN 0 85122 410 5 (hardback)
Printed by Warners of Bourne + London

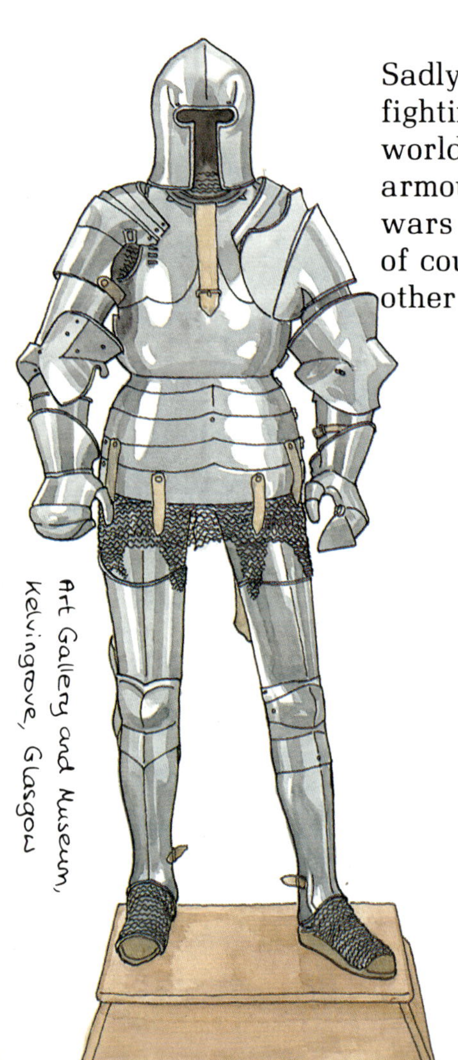

Sadly, people have been fighting each other since the world began. Weapons and armour used in battles and wars can be found in museums, of course, but also in many other surprising places.

Here is St George, with his visor up, on a stained glass window in a church.

Someone has even painted a crossed spear and bayonet on this plate. It was made to celebrate the French Revolution.

British Museum

About 2,600 years ago there were
women soldiers called Amazons.
They were tough fighters.
On this silver panel, an Amazon
is using a sling.

And here a Greek soldier and
an Amazon are fighting.

British Museum

On a pottery bowl
from Syria,
a knight in armour
gallops off
to battle.

People often used to ride into battle.
This stone panel tells part of the
story of an Assyrian battle about
2,700 years ago. Two soldiers are
riding on a camel. One uses his bow
and arrow, while the other beats the
camel with a stick to make it
go faster.

This Chinese painting shows a Mongol horseman from 500 years ago. His horse looks very different from the horses we know today.

An elephant carries soldiers to war in this picture from an 800-year-old manuscript.

At first, people only used helmets and shields to protect themselves.
The helmets were supposed to frighten the enemy too.

This Greek helmet, which is about 2,500 years old, looks a bit like a skull. The Greeks used bronze, made from mixing tin and copper, for their armour and weapons.

Here is a statue of a warrior from another part of the world at about the same time. This helmet would glint in the sun. Hundreds of them glinting together would look very frightening to the enemy.

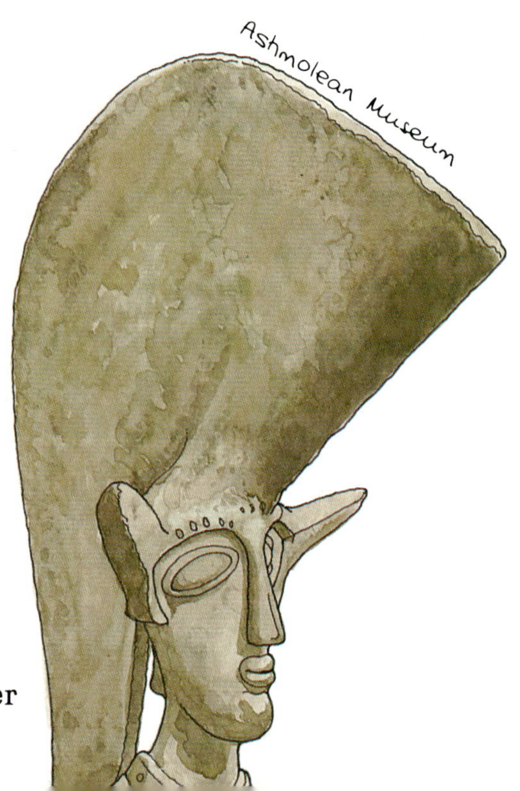

The wide flap on the back of
this Japanese helmet is to protect
the back of the neck. It would
have been hard to cut the
soldier's head off from behind.

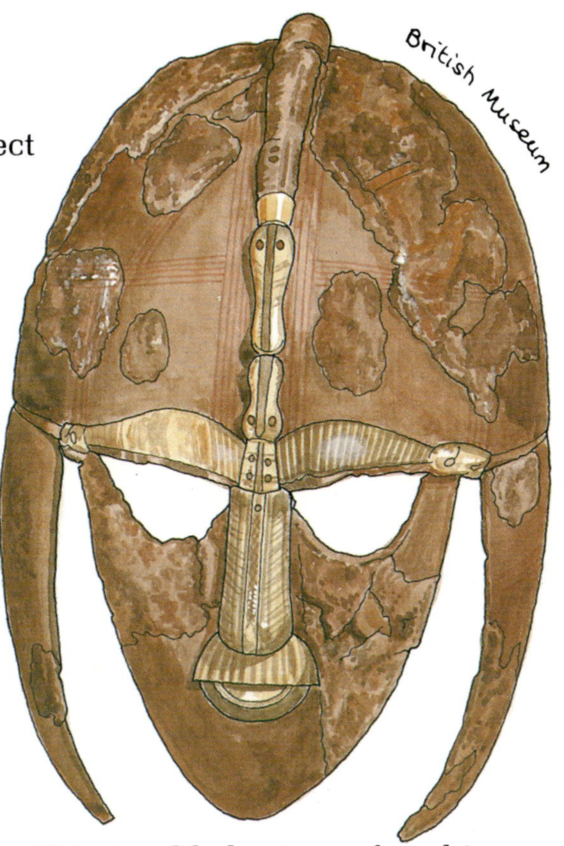

This royal helmet was found in
a ship burial in Britain. It is about
1,300 years old. For special
occasions, helmets were made of
gold, but on the battlefield
ordinary helmets of the same shape
were worn.

Later, as weapons became more dangerous, people protected themselves with full suits of armour. Look at brass tomb coverings to see how armour changed in 200 years.

A   In 1277 this knight wore chain mail.

B   About 50 years later, armour was made of iron plate.

C   And about 100 years after that, some soldiers had complete suits of plate. A sword could not pierce through the plate, but there had to be gaps in the plate so the man could move his limbs.

Many pictures in old books show armour. This picture of Richard II and his knights shows armour worn at the end of the 14th century.

In this 17th century Japanese manuscript a samurai wears traditional armour.

Art Gallery and Museum, Kelvingrove, Glasgow

This shield, called a *pavise*, was supposed to cover the whole body. It was used by a crossbowman in 1450. You can see the three swans and the sun's rays in the middle.

Japanese armour gradually became so richly decorated that it was very heavy to wear.

The craftsmen who made weapons
sometimes put their marks on them.

These flint daggers, used for
slashing and cutting, and made
in Scandinavia about 4,000
years ago, are too old to
have a mark on them.

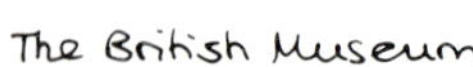

But on this Scottish sword,
which is about 200 years
old, the sword-maker's
mark shows a running
wolf.

Japanese swords often have cutting certificates marked on them. To test a sword, long ago, they used to try it out on the bodies of men who had been executed. Later, they used bundles of straw and bamboo.

How many swords can you count in this woodblock print?

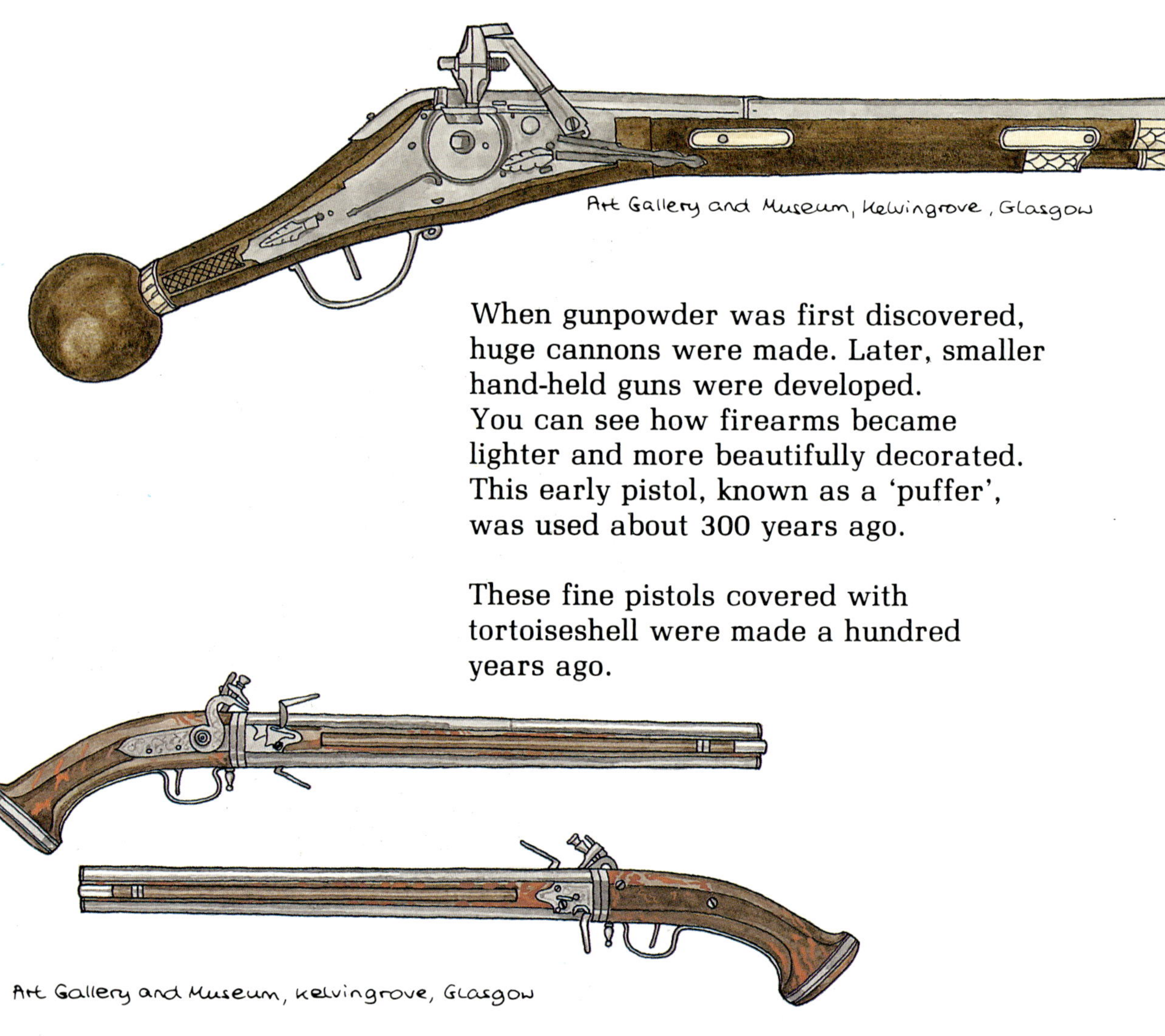

When gunpowder was first discovered,
huge cannons were made. Later, smaller
hand-held guns were developed.
You can see how firearms became
lighter and more beautifully decorated.
This early pistol, known as a 'puffer',
was used about 300 years ago.

These fine pistols covered with
tortoiseshell were made a hundred
years ago.

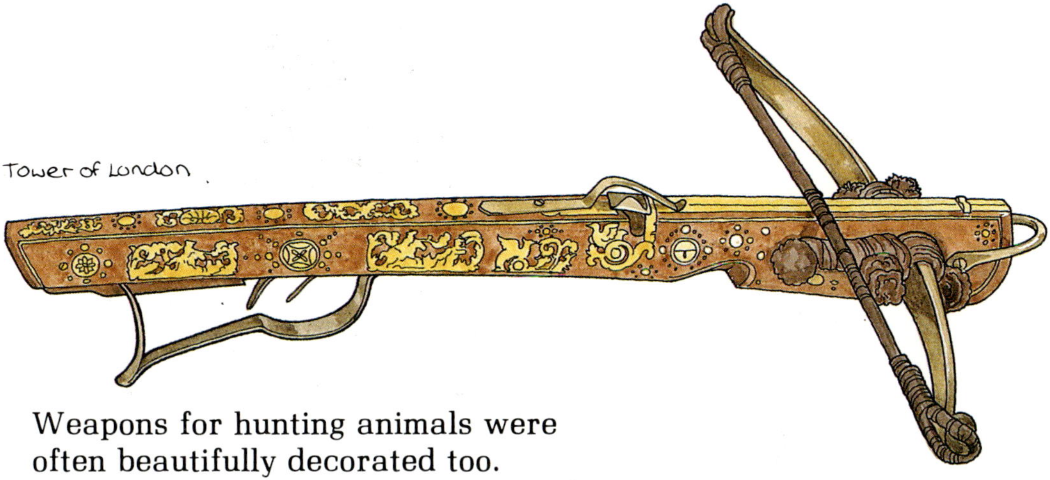

Weapons for hunting animals were
often beautifully decorated too.
Find the hunting scene on this crossbow,
made in Germany about 300 years ago.

The paws of a little lion are
the trigger of this crossbow.

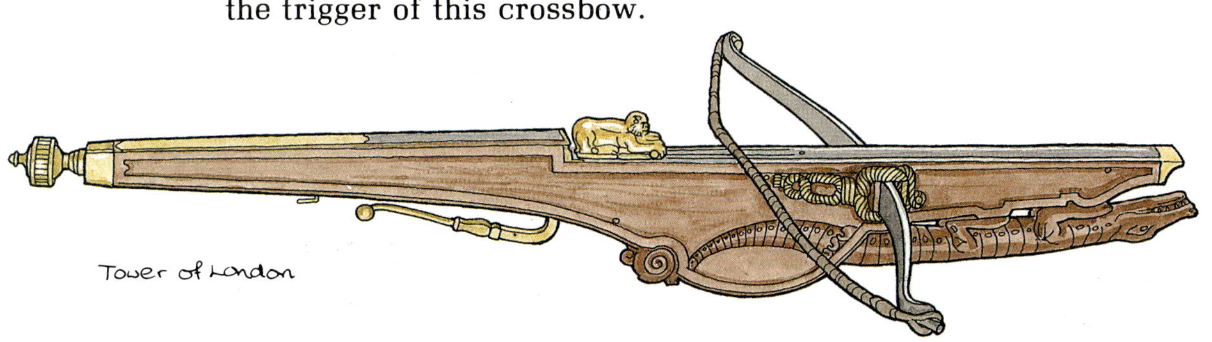

You can find out what happened to the hunted animals too. On a stone wall-carving about 2,700 years old, arrows have killed this lion.

The stag in this book illustration has just been shot by an archer.

The British Museum

A lioness is speared by hunters on an elephant in an Indian Mughal painting from about 400 years ago.

And another lioness is carried home.

War has always been very bloody. In this picture from a manuscript King Arthur beheads an enemy.

In an Indian book illustration, see the number of arms and legs that have been cut off.

On this stone wall painting, you can just see the heads of the enemy on the ground. A soldier is being given a bracelet to reward him for the number of heads he has cut off.

Private, Royal Army Medical Corps, 1914.

RAMC Historical Museum, Aldershot

Sometimes museums tell you how many people died in a particular battle. The numbers are horrifying. But it is quite difficult to find out what happened to the wounded soldiers— most of them probably died.

In 1415, only one cart was sent to the Battle of Agincourt for wounded men. But this painting shows that in 1914 the army had special horse-drawn carts and medical tents. Some of the horses had head-bells so that they sounded like battlefield ambulances.

Some paintings show the suffering of ordinary soldiers.
This 19th century painting shows a scene at the
Battle of Inkerman during the Crimean War.
The soldiers have little time to stop and help their
wounded friends.

Many towns and villages in Britain have a statue or other memorial carved with the names of the local men who were killed in the First or Second World War.

These are sad to read, as often many men with the same surname are listed, and this may mean that a woman lost her husband, brother and son.

Bethnal Green Museum of Childhood

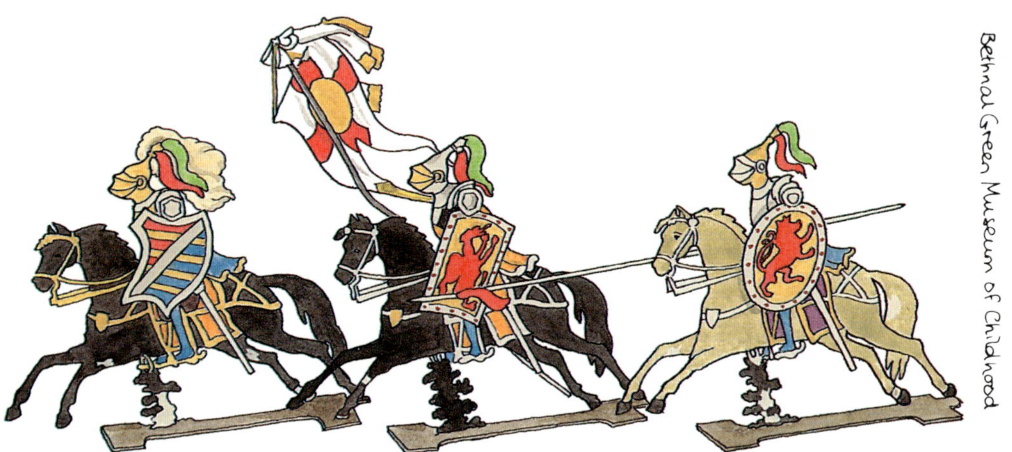

But it is always fun to look at models of soldiers.
Here some knights ride off to the crusades.

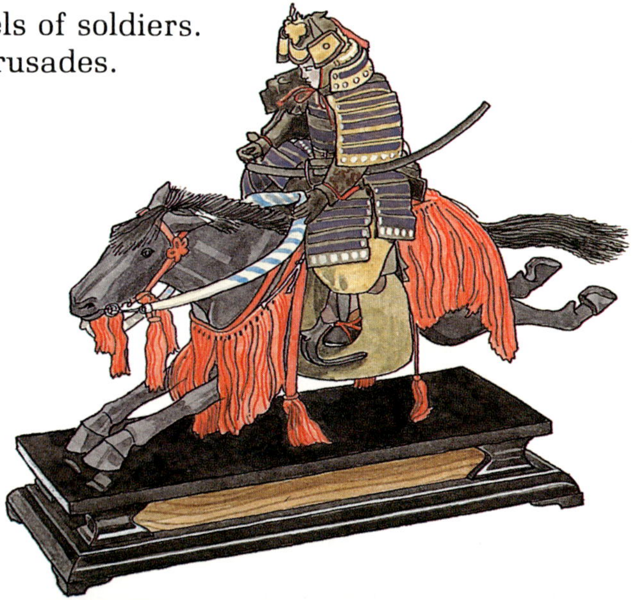

And this is a Japanese warrior.

Here are some soldiers from the First World War.

And this model of a British officer
was made in Germany in 1914.

Instead of just looking at weapons, remember to look in other places for signs of war and battle.

This medal was given to the commanders of the English fleet after a war against the Dutch 300 years ago.

Ashmolean Museum

And don't be surprised if you find odd things in the shape of soldiers. These nutcrackers are about 200 years old!

Bethnal Green Museum of Childhood

You can find lots more 'blood and thunder' too.
Why not make your own book and draw pictures of
some of the things you find when you are out?
Write some notes about where they come from,
what they were used for, when they were made, and
where you saw them.

Here are some of the places to remember to look:

War memorials in towns and churches
Old books and manuscripts
Toy collections and model collections
Museums   China dishes
Paintings   Tombstones
Coins   Stained glass windows
Medals